We Meet Again

Savita Nair

Leadstart
INKSTATE

ISBN 978-93-5458-050-5
Copyright © Savita Nair, 2021

First published in India 2021 by Leadstart Inkstate
A Division of One Point Six Technologies Pvt Ltd

119-123, 1st Floor, Building J2, B - Wing,
Wadala Truck Terminal, Wadala East,
Mumbai 400022, Maharashtra, INDIA
Phone: +91 96999 33000
Email: info@leadstartcorp.com
www.leadstartcorp.com

Disclaimer: The views expressed in this book are those of the Author and do not pertain to be held by the Publisher.

Editor: Vaibhav Pathare
Cover: R. Maharaja
Layouts: Kshitij Dhawale

To Papa,
Thank you for your patience

About the Author

Savita Nair is a self-confessed 'indulgent' poet. Having spent most of her years as an advertising copywriter, she finds writing poetry works as a balm to soothe her frayed 'advertising nerves'. Like several other poets, she claims that there are days when nothing eclectic enters her thoughts. And then there are those 'inspired' days when everything mundane, turns into prose. Savita lives for those days.

The author now resides in Pune and spends her time consulting on brands - interspersed with bouts of poetry writing and self-doubting. Her deep-rooted curiosity in people is what keeps her going - in life and work. She loves to know what makes people tick or tock, why they think what they do and essentially why everyone is so flawed yet fascinating.

When she is not writing poems, ads, or songs, Savita is sipping wine, trying to keep up hopelessly with Instagram trends or dreaming of places to travel to.

Contents

WE MEET AGAIN

Once again, I want to tell you about my mind
And how they spill with thoughts
Once again, I want to create a space in your head
With all the memories I've brought.

Once again, I want to fall in love with you
And hope you feel the same
Once again, I want to share a song about courage
And a poem or two on shame.

Once again, I want you in my reverie
So, you know what my silences mean
Once again, I want us to sigh and smile
About all that, we could've done and been.

Once again, I want us to break the walls
That make us strangers in conversation
Once again, I want us to connect in ways
That don't suffer from familiar stagnation.

My friend, here we are again
I guess it isn't goodbye
So, let's find a place where it's not so rushed
And we can begin with You and I.

I'M NOT OKAY WITH THAT

I think you may find I don't fit in
And I'm okay with that
But don't try to prescribe a 'simple' solution
I'm not okay with that.

I think you may find I don't subscribe to most views
And I'm okay with that
But don't tell me I don't care at all
I'm not okay with that.

I think you may find me rude and outspoken
And I'm okay with that
But don't expect me to share a sad story
I'm not okay with that.

I think you may want me to be loud and brazen
And I'm okay with that
But don't tell me that I need to take a side
I'm not okay with that.

I think you may like me selectively
And I'm okay with that
But don't ask me to select you to be liked
I'm not okay with that.

I think you may find I'm part of this world's 'uncool' and 'unseen'
And I'm okay with that
But don't twist me around to suit your narrative
I'm not okay with that.

THE MISTAKES WE MAKE, MAKE US

We went wrong
We went right
We shed tears
Without putting up a fight
Will we mend our ways?
Maybe not.
Because the mistakes we made
Made us.

We shoved people away
Then we clung to what didn't matter
We wanted to belong
So, we pretended to love the chatter
Will we mend our ways?
Maybe not.
Because the mistakes we made
Made us.

We thought we had conviction
Then we sold our souls
We fought a loud battle
Because someone poked holes

Will we mend our ways?
Maybe not.
Because the mistakes we made
Made us.

We sheltered those we love
Expecting them to feel the same
And when they distanced us
We called them nothing but lame
Will we mend our ways?
Maybe not.
Because the mistakes we made
Made us.

Mistakes.
They're like wounds.
The deeper you make one
The more it bleeds
The more it stays with you.
The more it shapes you
In good ways and bad
We make mistakes.
Mistakes make us.

I MEET PEOPLE ALL THE TIME

I meet people all the time
Some of them are scared of what will happen
If people 'find out'
And they will always continue to be
Some of them say they don't care at all
When they're the most affected
Some, pretend to be who they're not
And that robs them of their charm
And then some... really aren't there
They're not anywhere
Not with me or you.
Because they've died within
And haven't left a clue.

I meet people all the time
Some of them are so happy
It makes you cry
And you hope it all stays that way
Some of them are just angry
And they've lost all idea
About what or why
And then there are those
Who are plain spiteful

Because it makes them believe
That they've done their bit
To save the world
Are there are those who want to change
Not for others, for themselves
They aren't afraid of it
Because to change is difficult
And we all need to.

I meet people all the time
Some of them follow others
Because safety lies in numbers
And why stick out?
Some of them are rebels
And that's a good thing
But then they stretch it too far
Some of them are fanatic
And I have reason to believe
They're obnoxious
And then there are some
Who shake off the system
And the code of right and wrong
Living a life, they believe is happy
Because as long as they don't hurt anyone
It's all good.
I like such people.
I meet people all the time.

A STRANGE DAY OF CALM

The sun won't be our best friend today
The tea may just run cold
But if you'll play me a tune that's mellow
I can't say I won't be sold
There's a song that I want to sing
About tea cake and such merry things
For today's not a day to be upset
Because it's not that kind of day
So, let's not forget.

The fan is whirring a bit too loud
The clothes are hanging out to dry
And even when you say they'll be okay
I'm fretting about it being a lie
There's tonnes of stuff that we lack
But then my worries just fade to black
For today's not a day to fret
Because it's not that kind of day
So, let's not sweat.

The mess around us won't be gone too soon
The trips we planned may be on hold
And even as our lives assume the New Normal
We'll feel we're just so controlled
The present has this habit of wavering
And our luck may seem unfavouring
But today's not a day for regrets
Because it's not that kind of day
So, let's place our bets.

EXCEPT, ESPECIALLY

I remember the day
When you sang me a song
You were struggling to remember the words
And your tune was woeful
Everything was less than perfect
Except for the way you looked at me
Everything was more than perfect
Especially when you looked at me.

I remember the day
When you brought me breakfast in bed
The toast was overdone
And the eggs were a bit under
Everything was less than perfect
Except for the way you smiled with me
Everything was more than perfect
Especially when you smiled with me.

I remember the day
When our worlds stopped ticking together
The tunes seemed strangely incongruous
The breakfast, strangely bland
Everything was less than perfect
Except for the tears in my eyes, that day
Everything was more than perfect
Especially when I wiped my tears away.

WINE AND CIGARETTES

All the music has faded
And there's nothing but the sound
Of a bottle touching the table
And an ashtray going around
We're ready to call it a night
And yet, it's just 3 am
There's a lot that's left unsaid
In the words and silences between them
Find out more about me
Tell me things that I should know
And if you want to drop your guard
Succumb and I'll follow.

Chaos is just a matter of mind
Still it, and you'll find
There's a new world in my head that's forming
Of leaving this one behind
I see us smiling at a rainbow
With not a care and zero regrets
But maybe, that's just fascination built
On thought and wine and cigarettes.

In your eyes, I see new intensity
In mine, I see new affection
And as dawn starts to unfold
I discover a new connection
There's no safety in saying nothing
There's no bravado in saying it all
But there's the distinct possibility
Of mending fences, breaking walls
Again and again, the clock has chimed
And orange is the colour of the sky
The Sun may not appear so soon
For the moon is hesitant to say goodbye.

Chaos is just a matter of mind
Still it, and you'll find
There's a new world in my head that's forming
Of leaving this one behind
I see us smiling at a rainbow
With not a care and zero regrets
But maybe, that's just fascination built
On thought and wine and cigarettes.

DOING THE BEST WE CAN

We can go round and round
And come to the same conclusion
We can take everything as it comes
And further add to the confusion
We can discuss things to death
And worry ourselves to a point of no return
We can throw caution to the wind
And watch one another bruise and burn
There's no right or wrong answer
There's no Yes or No plan
There's just a sense of knowing
That we're doing the best we can.

We can fall back on our old habits
And find that we're fed up and tired
We can pick up the pieces and start again
And see if we're differently wired
We can let our shadows haunt us
And create a narrative quite frightening
We can light a candle in the dark
And find the prospect enlightening
There's no good or bad reason
There's no lesser or greater than
There's just a sense of knowing
That we're doing the best we can.

We can shake up the constant
And make changes work in our favour
We can hold ourselves accountable
And emerge a whole lot braver
We can seal it all with a kiss
And carry the memories to our grave
We can shove it all below the carpet
And make regret our only slave
There's no bright or dull moment
There's no lesser woman or man
There's just a sense of knowing
That we're doing the best we can.

A POEM ABOUT HER

She'll kiss the storm
Because she kicked it up
Then break her heart
Not knowing how to pick it up
She'll burn a hole
Because she thinks she can
Then try and stitch it up
To end up where she began
This is not her story
This is not her song
This is not her right
This is not her wrong
This is the life
She's lived far too long
This is the life
She's lived far too long.

She'll make a deal
Then question it again
She'll throw in her cards
When she stands to gain
She'll quit the game
Just as it was going her way
Then find herself at crossroads

That lead to a cliché
This is not her yin
This is not her yang
This is not her pain
This is not her pang
This is the life
She's made into her plan
This is the life
She's made into her plan.

She'll find the answers
To questions in her head
Then she'll question the answers
To find what lies ahead
She'll catch a glimpse of the sun
And bask in its shine
Then relish the rain
As if it were wine
This is not her show
This is not her sell
This is not her sin
This is not her hell
This is the life
She's born to tell
This is the life
She's born to tell.

RUN AWAY WITH ME

Heady days and hedonistic nights
Were never out of question
But the balminess of these moments
Were filled with trepidation.
Everything that's sugar coated
May not be your cup of tea
Everything that's as honest as day
May not agree with me.
There's not a thing we now agree on
There's not a thing we can do jointly
But that's the thing about running away
You can still run away from me.

Defiant times and defying stereotypes
We agreed on things like those
But we were weird-ed out by the ordinary
So there we stood, exposed.
Everything we had fought for
May not have been a battle of consequence
Everything that we glossed over
May just have had bigger significance.
There's not a thing we now agree on
There's not a thing we can do jointly
But that's the thing about running away
You can still run away with me.

Sometime in life, we'll look back and think
If we tried enough or stayed in-between
Then we'll un-crowd our heart by saying again
That the other one lost the sheen.
There's not a thing we will agree on
There's not a thing we will do jointly
And yet, when it comes to running away
You can still run away with me.

BRAND-NEW DAY

You and me and the sky
   We made a tryst to love each other
And then the sea intervened
So, we decided to share secrets together
The sky and the sea are still out there
Waiting to hear us say
Let's start again where we left off
Let's make it a brand-new day.

You and me and the trees
We could listen to each other sighing
And then the birds chirped in
We were no longer scared of flying
The trees and the birds are patient
They'll wait for us to be brave
Let's take this out in the open
Let's make it a brand-new day.

You and me and the rainfall
We would often exchange more than news
And then the puddles started laughing
For they wanted us to break loose
The puddles and the rain will miss us
If we could only find a way
Let's change the stagnancy of the present
Let's make it a brand-new day.

WHAT HAVE YOU

There's someone who's distracting
And someone who's distracted
There's someone who's attracting
And someone's who's attracted
When you're sitting at home, thinking up things
Who's to say you've not over-reacted.
Who's to say there's not a table
Laid out just for two
Roses and music and well,
What have you.

There's a tune playing somewhere
And one playing just for you
There's a film you think is brilliant
And one you can't get through
When your mind is both full and empty
Who's to say what rings as true.
Who's to say there's not a journey
To which, you haven't got a clue
With twists and turns and well,
What have you.

There's a conversation that's started
And you feel you can change its course
There's someone who's decided to ghost you
And you feel not a pinch of remorse
When everything around is moving steadily
Who's to say you can't apply force
Who's to say, you're not that bolt
That strikes out of the blue
Who burns and stings and well,
What have you.

FOR ME, IT'S HEAVEN

I have a corner I call mine
It's by the window
And it doesn't come with a great view
But there's some sunshine streaming in
And for me, that seems like
Heaven.

I have a kitchen, not too big
It's got no fancy gadgets
In fact, the roof is leaky
But I've had some great conversations here
And for me, that seems like
Heaven.

I have a money plant in a bottle
A bottle of gin that I drank all of
The plant itself may not grow
But perhaps, it's stronger that I think
And for me, that seems like
Heaven.

I have a lampshade by my bed
It's old and has seen better days
Not too big, not too pretty
But its light is all things mellow
And for me, that seems like
Heaven.

I have a coffee mug that I drink out of
It's been used and reused way too often
And maybe it needs to retire
But maybe it needs another coffee
And for me, that seems like
Heaven.

I have a corner I call mine
It's by the window
And it doesn't come with a great view
But there's some sunshine streaming in
And for me, that seems like
Heaven.

SERIOUSLY, I'M ALIVE

Seriously, I'm alive.

Though I hardly ever feel the sun beating down on me
Or see my furniture arranged differently
But seriously, I'm alive.

Though my days are mundanely absurd
And news floating around me is way too disturbed
But seriously, I'm alive.

The metaphorical masks we wore, have a literal version too
And about things like travel and wine, we no longer have a clue
But seriously, I'm alive.

Who can say what's the end and what's the beginning
Who's doing the right thing now, who's sinning
But seriously, I'm alive.

Religion is still playing it's best card, and we're game
Stigmas still abound, we should hang our heads in shame
But seriously, I'm alive.

This battle may end, but at what cost?
We may gain perspective, but how many lives lost?

Seriously, I'm alive?

END OF YEAR, START OF HERE

Find a shoe that fits
Find a shirt that's nice
Place your bets on that drink
Tone up your jokes with spice.

A new year may not be a big change
And yet, it may be a good turn
To do things a little differently
And settle those tears and burn.

It's not a great resolution
But great isn't always ours to do
Make a slight calibration
Turquoise is better than blue.

All that we do comes with reasoning
And sometimes, no reason at all
The edge may be closer than you think
The cracks will show in that wall.

So, let the sunshine in without brakes
Let the rain in without the gates
This is our goodbye to the mess gone by
This is our Hello to the mess that awaits.

TAKE YOUR TIME

Take your time
We're not going anywhere soon
We're just going to enjoy our noon
For the night is bound to be young
And we won't leave any dream unsung
So, take your time
For what more can we afford
But time.

Take your time
There's a lot of chaos everywhere
And this world, it will never be fair
There's not a whole lot we can do
Except try and keep things new
So, take your time
For our worlds will finally collide
In good time.

Take your time
They say all it takes is a start
And a fire burning in your heart
We may never know what could've been
If our tomorrows were aquamarine

So, take your time
For what is gratitude if not measured
With time.

Take your time
Away and away we shall go
Shedding the fast, kissing the slow
It'll all be reminiscent
Of what was said and truly meant
So, take your time
For what we know is this
This is our time.

QUANTUM LEAP

Grey areas
And those fly-by-night ideas
Blind spots
And losing battles fought
Immature reactions
And those hasty actions
Fearless sins
And greedy compromised wins
They gouge our conscience
And cut through our sleep
They singe our souls
Then beg us to weep
This is the Phantom
Of selling out cheap
This is the Phantom
Of taking a Quantum Leap.

Knives drawn
And those memories far gone
Feelings entangled
And nerves quite jangled
Incessant questioning
And those standards quite lessening
Wounds reopened

And promises left broken
They shake our beliefs
And shake our convictions
They make us slaves
Of perilous deviations
This is the Phantom
Of selling out cheap
This is the Phantom
Of taking a Quantum Leap.

Extended lifelines
And those half-bleeding deadlines
Tiresome lies
And easy-to-break ties
Lackluster efforts
And those puerile comforts
Fallible souls
And those ever-altering goals
They bind us to something
And take everything in return
They light a thousand lamps
Yet in darkness, we burn
This is the Phantom
Of selling out cheap
This is the Phantom
Of taking a Quantum Leap.

LIFE IS COMING FOR YOU

We aren't made with endless bridges of hope
Neither are we filled with stagnant buckets of mope.

We're just a juxtaposition of tiny jumbles
We build and then quickly crumble.

We're strong and yet so feeble
We're vile and yet so agreeable.

We can be shaken and stay resolute
We can be vague and turn absolute.

We may be mean and still disarming
We may be chaotic and still be calming.

We hold the potential of worst and best
We live the extremes of peace and unrest.

Yes, we may falter, with every blow
Yes, we may alter, each time we glow.

Yes, we'll go through the days where we succumb
Yes, we'll have those days of playing dumb.

Sure, we'll end up vanquished and then some more
Sure, we'll find a day when we bounce back to keep score.

This is never going to be easy, but you knew it
This may not be too clean, but you'll never rue it.

So take that sword, take that bandage too
Make a clean break, find a fresh glue
It's not a now-or-never situation that you need to work
It's a lifetime of decisions that you cannot shirk.

Are you listening, are you ready to make new
For even if you're not, life is coming for you..

VIEWFINDER

I want to find a view
That's different and new
But each time I look out
I seek what I already knew.

I want to find a view
That's uncluttered and unfiltered
But since I haven't seen much of that
My eyes are left bewildered.

I want to find a view
That can show me what I've been missing
But there's a sceptic who's yawning within
And saying, that's just a blessing.

I want to find a view
That has the power to create more joy
But my mind turns into a roadblock
And warns me of my will to destroy.

I want to find a view
That's weird and yet, makes sense
But then, I start to piece things together
And commit my biggest offence.

I want to find a view
That will help me find what's ideal
Then it hits me and I realize quite late
That only I can keep it real.

TIME GOES BY

Ages, it's been ages
Since we shared a cuppa tea
And it's been even longer since we just met
For the magic of each other's company.

Years, it's been years
Since we cut down on the pleasantries
And exchanged views that are soaked in
The rawness of uncertainties.

Months, it's been months
Since we left our phones behind
And broke down the walls that bind us
In the recesses of our too-busy mind.

Weeks, it's been weeks
Since we stayed true to who we were
And did exactly what we dared to do
When our hearts were still amateur.

Days, it's been days
Since we said the simplest words
Not the stuff we pass off as conversation now
Because deep down, we're just cowards.

Moments, it's been moments
Since we took a deeper breath
Because sooner than later, it'll feel like
We've been living an age of death.

TOUGHER THAN YOU SHOW

You keep taking the fall
Risking it all
And marching on with wounds within you
You keep flashing that smile
Lasting the mile
And settling for things that belittle you.

People say you're winning
When you think you're waning
People think you're daring
When you think you're despairing
But maybe people are right
Maybe you still have the fight
And you can still take the blow
Maybe there's a truth only they know.

Sister, sit up and listen
You're tougher than you show.
You're tougher than you show.

You make the same mistakes
Live life without brakes
And blame no one else besides you
You get shaken to the core
But you still long for more
Because there's a sadist begging inside you.

People say you're feisty
When you think you're hasty
People say you're radical
When you think you're whimsical
But maybe people are right
Maybe you still have the fight
And you can still take the blow
Maybe there's a truth only they know.

Sister, sit up and listen
You're tougher than you show.
You're tougher than you show.

You have no real purpose
Because life has been a circus
It's just that you're tired being the same old you
You don't want to live on a whim
Because it's starting to look quite dim
It's sad that no one else believes that but you.

People say you're merry
When you think you're ordinary
People say you're crazy
But you think you're a bit hazy
But maybe people are right
Maybe you still have the fight
And you can still take the blow
Maybe there's a truth only they know.

Sister, sit up and listen
You're tougher than you show
You're tougher than you show.

WHAT WE MUST KNOW

You've been saying a lot of things
But try saying what you mean
The filter you use when you speak
It's a coating, much like polythene.

Every word is protected against opinion
Every line is missing a viewpoint
Everything you say hits just the right note
And yet, everything is structured to disappoint.

No one is minus flaws or scars
No one has lived a life harmonious
We all break down and show our fears
We all say things that are erroneous.

Shame and punishment will co-exist
As will self-destruction and self-pity
When we decide, that we choose to un-hide
Is when we will live a life more gritty.

There isn't a problem with niceness
Or with angst or with outrage
What we must know, is the further we go
Our souls will loathe this gilded cage.

THE HOUSE ON THE TREE

There stands a house, on top of a tree
Made of sticks and stones, and honesty
It's not all that perfect, but it's got the sky
Looking down at me, asking me why
Why I'm tired, why I sound so weary
And whether I'd like to just climb a tree.

There stands a house, on top of a tree
Shrouded from the grimness of reality
It squeaks and it grunts, as I get inside
It says to me, come sit and confide
Be who you were, when you were young and free
When all you wanted was to just climb a tree.

There stands a house, on top of a tree
Designed by nature, known only to me
It's got two cushions, cheerful but frayed
And a warm blanket, for when I'm afraid
And a kettle that's just right to make a pot of tea
For the days when you simply wish to climb a tree.

There stands a house, on top of a tree
No one has been there, not even me
I think of it often, but there's a lot on my mind
And ever so often, it's what I've left behind
And while I continue to be a child of apathy
I look back at the wonder of just climbing a tree.

A LATE REALIZATION

You jump into a storm
And escape it narrowly
You say you'll be more careful
Then jump straight into the sea
You step into a tornado
Then claim you'll take it easy
But you go and undo everything
By overdoing lazy
Your problem isn't you're no good
Your problem is you think you're best
If you just stuck to being better
You'd probably have lasted the test

I'm no good at being Agony Aunt
Or giving worldly advice
But I've erred enough to know this much
We each will pay the price.
One can't be the sweetheart
And the sinner and the clown
One can't climb a wall, then walk on edge
And shudder when you look down.

You claim to be the misfit
Then desire to be accepted
You wear the garb of indifference
Then retreat when you're neglected
You're looking back at the shadows
Then looking up at the Sun
And when you look at your reflection
You're honestly close to done
Your problem isn't that you know nothing
Your problem is that you know far too much
And if you just left all that bravado behind
You'd realize the power of Touch.

I'm no good at playing earnest
Or winning someone's heart
But I've done enough to ensure I won't
Top the popularity chart.
One can't be the lover
And the loser and the saint
One can't open up one's heart and then
Cover it with a coat of paint.

OUR CHOICES

Some left us wiser
Some left us scarred
Some didn't even better
Our moral scorecard
Then we continued to look back
Then we continued to wonder
If the repercussions were born
Out of a boon or a blunder.

Our Choices, our Choices
The ones that turned into our bold new voices
The ones that faded into unsure decisions
The ones that underwent a thousand revisions
The ones that paved the half-lit way
The ones that made us what we are today.
Our Choices, our Choices
Some half-tears, some near-rejoices
The ones that made us silly and afraid
The ones that left us feeble and frayed
The ones that shaped our all-too-brave actions
The ones that became chain reactions

Some made us look back
Others forced us to look ahead
Some brought us alive
Some rendered us half-dead
Then we continued to battle
With the what-ifs and what-nots
As we tried to piece the past
And struggled to connect the dots.

Our Choices, our Choices
The ones that turned into our bold new voices
The ones that morphed into unsure decisions
The ones that underwent a thousand revisions
The ones that paved the half-lit way
The ones that made us what we are today.
Our Choices, our Choices
Some half-tears, some near-rejoices
The ones that made us silly and afraid
The ones that left us feeble and frayed
The ones that shaped our all-too-brave actions
The ones that became chain reactions.

WE WERE, WE ARE

We used to dive without fear
In the sea of love and defiance
Today we're happy wetting our feet
In the shores of commonplace compliance.

We used to write love stories
The kind that would ravage us from within
Today our love is battered by reality
And our reality is coated with sin.

We used to make mistakes
And swear we'd never repeat them again
Today we repeat them to find release
In the haunting pleasure of pain.

We used to share the stories
The stories that were simple, yet strong
Today our stories are numbed by the hypocrisy
That comes from playing along.

We used to have a life
One, defined by the thrill of adventure
Today, it's defined by the goals we've set
And punctuated by society's cruel censure.

Oh the days, they pass us by and yet
Each day comes with the reckoning
That the best has passed, the goodness won't last
And yet, there's a storm that's beckoning.

SOME OF THIS, SUM OF THAT

There's a home-bird inside of me
Who dreams of taking the next flight out
There's brilliance seated deep within
But my mediocrity is what starts to shout
There's randomness that's volcanic, outpouring
Then there's OCD that simmers inside
There's a composure that few can fathom
And a gloss that's loudly magnified
There's the poet that's part of the picture
And the dancer who's looking for a tune
There's a joker who can't keep a straight face
And a cynic who's bored too soon.

This and that
That and this
We're some of all
We're a sum of all
Some parts enthralling
Some parts not at all
A river can't always live
Like a waterfall.

Rainfall brings out the melancholic
But sunshine rests easy on my search for hope
Sarcasm is a robust remedy I use
When sincerity finds little scope
Strength is a last-minute reserve, best guarded
Because it seldom pays to be vulnerable
Bold is a way of life I choose
Though blushing suits me, just as well.
The swish of a restaurant menu is fascinating
And so is the comfort of home food
There's love that craftily knocks at my heart
Then there's the call of solitude.

This and that
That and this
We're some of all
We're a sum of all
Some parts enthralling
Some parts not at all
A river can't always live
Like a waterfall.

I WILL LIVE IN YOU

When words are just pretty little accessories
And you feel the need to soak in raw silence
When your vivid travel stories take you nowhere
And you desperately feel the need to find a balance
When your hopelessness is like a backpack that won't close
And you want to sit down and unpack it all
When your mates look like shiny medals in an oasis of success
And you strangely feel much too small.

Remember me then
For I'd rather be with you at that time
When your mind needs the healing
When your heart craves for feeling
When nothing makes too much sense
When you'd rather see life through my lens
Remember me then
For I will live in you.

When the most stylish restaurants are mere excuses
For you to add time to your calendar of pretend-arrogance
When the dresses and the shoes and privileges and jazz
Are softly, crying out your lack of inner elegance
When your kindness is a concept, not an action or a thought

When your generosity, with selfishness is fraught
When each day weighs upon you like a disease with no cure
And you finally come to realize, happiness can seldom be bought.

Remember me then
For I'd rather be with you at that time
When your demeanor is gentle and meek
When your actions far loudly speak
When fake bravado is sold or discarded
When all duality is staunchly disregarded
Remember me then
For I will live in you.

THE SPIN

I didn't expect to linger so long
But the night just grew on me
We hadn't planned to drink as much
But it all flowed naturally.

The music wasn't too loud and then
There was that sudden burst of rain
And just like that, the stars went black
And your smile felt like champagne.

It's a crazy world, I do believe
And all we can do is spin
But when we stop, we shall not wait
For another ride to begin.

Content is an uncommon feeling
For those who've been restless for a while
But I can see that I may change
If you'll make it all worthwhile.

We're not made of blood and bones
We're made of breathless passion
We're not made of reason and rhyme
We're made in a careless fashion.

It's a crazy world, I do believe
And all we can do is spin
But when we stop, we will not wait
For another ride to begin.

THAT KIND OF DAY

It's that kind of day
When our hearts should do the talking
And the head must take a sabbatical.

It's that kind of day
When grey and green should marry
And paint the landscape with thoughts irrational.

It's that kind of day
When small talk should be nipped in the bud
And conversations should foster on wine.

It's that kind of day
When wishes should be granted on a whim
And logic should be entrapped in a shrine.

It's that kind of day
When memories should be the stairway to magic
And magic should be the default state of mind.

It's that kind of day
When actions shouldn't seek explanation
And ideas should play unconfined.

It's that kind of day
When delight should be kissed by impulse
And feelings should embrace poor judgment.

It's that kind of day
When the sea and sky must be our mates
And our compass must be abandonment.

LOSING THE PLOT

Here's to the criticized lot
Who oftentimes, lose the plot.

Who laugh and cry with amplified abandon
Whose actions are questionable, random.

Who overdo feelings, overdo their drinking
Who love like mad, without much thinking.

Who part with money, don't part with people
Who write their story, without planning a sequel.

Who say what comes to mind, without context
Who put their cards on the table for a zero prospect.

Who have no agenda, since it holds no attraction
Who give it all up for a friend, then get a fraction.

Who repent and burn, for the mistakes they've made
Then they repeat the same, naïve yet unafraid.

Who share their food, their homes, their madness
Who'll hold you close with both joy and sadness.

They're not mavericks, they're not misfits
They're not silly or weird or taboo
Because when it comes to losing the plot
It could well be Me and You.

THE TRUTH BEHIND SIMPLE

We all stay simple
Till we get horribly entwined
In empty words and forgotten promises
And ideologies that render us blind.

We all stay simple
Till we second-guess what others are thinking
Then we worry double, invite more trouble
And the result is a morale that's sinking.

We all stay simple
Till we wonder if we're as important as we appear
Then we work hard to prove it, even over-prove it
And in the bargain, all that remains is fear.

We all stay simple
Till we figure we've not earned as much as we wanted
Then we desperately flutter and fly
And for years, we stay hunted and haunted.

We all stay simple
Till our greed to take charge becomes overwhelming
Humane is lost, human is left
The shame that remains is far from compelling.

We all stay simple
Till we aren't and we wish that we were
But no matter what we say, the truth on any given day
Complicated is what we prefer.

WALK THE TALK

Promises sound good in advertising
And probably in a love song, devout
But when it comes to the acid test
I'd request you to cut them out
Substituting words for action is like
Substituting soya for meat
What I mean to say and I mean this well
That a cheat is a cheat is a cheat
As you get older, face up to this
That your words may flow round-the-clock
But when it comes to being a better man
You've just got to walk the talk.

Talking the walk is your strong suit
Walking the talk is your Achilles' heel
And finally, it will all come down to this
Are you the real deal?
It's not so easy, it's not so hard
It just requires you to act how you feel
Because finally, it will all come down to this
Are you the real deal?

Being a tease is somewhat interesting
When you're at the bar, giggling madly
But when it comes to sustaining my interest
I must admit you're doing badly
Flirty promises are fun, but will they last
That's like asking if peacocks are useful
What I mean to say, is that after some time
They bore me to tears, to be truthful.
As you get older, face up to this
That your cuteness can flow, round-the-clock
But when it comes to being a better woman
You've just got to walk the talk.

Talking the walk is your strong suit
Walking the talk is your Achilles' heel
And finally, it will all come down to this
Are you the real deal?
It's not so easy, it's not so hard
It just requires you to act how you feel
Because finally, it will all come down to this
Are you the real deal?

THE ONE WHO GOT AWAY

The look in your eyes
Tells me you think I'm not the one
The tone in your voice
Tells me you think I'm just good fun
Hold on to the thought
That thought won't go just as yet
But years, many years later
You'll look back to when we met
And wonder if this was just
A fleeting look at the sun
Butterflies don't happen in a trice
Silk needs time to be spun.

The one who got away
I'll be the one who got away
The one who defied the cliché
I'll be the one who got away
The one who got away
I'll be the one who got away
Retrospection is just a person
Who's lived an extra day.

The delays in your response
Tells me you've taken me for granted
The sting in your nonchalance
Tells me you're disenchanted
Hold on to the limbo
The limbo won't shake off just yet
But years, many years later
You'll look back with a tinge of regret
And wonder if you'd written the song
With a fresh new tune in mind
Because even rhapsodies start off
As melodies unrefined.

The one who got away
I'll be the one who got away
Defying every cliché
I'll be the one who got away
The one who got away
I'll be the one who got away
Retrospection is just a person
Who's lived an extra day.

UPPER DOWNER

She's been up all night
Getting rather trashed
She's still awake now
Sweetly unabashed
Then you tell her to behave
And she quietly nods her head
She smiles and oh, it's a trip
One that you love, you dread
This is that smile
That smile that brought you closer
This is that smile
That smile that says it's over
This is that smile
That smile that abuses you slowly
And yet, this is that smile
That smile that seduces you wholly.

Upper Downer
She'll take you in, then throw you out
Upper Downer
It's that fix you can't do without
Upper Downer
You want to soar, you want to dive
Upper Downer
You feel so dead, yet so alive.

He's shaken off the memory
That he's made with her
He's taking off again
Because he won't do forever
Then you'll tell him to slow down
And he'll shyly ask you why
He smiles and oh, it's a trip
It makes you smile, then cry
This is that smile
That smile that feels like a rush
This is that smile
That smile that turns you to mush
This is that smile
That smile that makes you believe
And yet, this is that smile
That smile that can fully deceive.

Upper Downer
He'll take you in, then throw you out
Upper Downer
It's that fix you can't do without
Upper Downer
You want to soar, you want to dive
Upper Downer
You feel so dead, yet so alive.

NORMAL IS WHO YOU ARE

They judged him
Because he wasn't like the rest
Maybe because he didn't fit in
He didn't care so much to be the best
All he wanted was to potter around
And flit around like the butterflies
Sit amongst books and dolls and such
Then wonder idly at the expansive skies
"Why can't he be normal?" they asked
But the answer wasn't one they agreed upon
So, they made him an object of their ridicule
While he stood in a corner, forlorn.

They judged her
Because she wasn't just like every other
Maybe she was too much of a wallflower
She certainly wasn't as pretty as her mother
Her comfort lay in numbers and codes
And theories that were not accidental
All she wanted was to understand the cosmos
In a way that would prove elemental
"Why can't she be normal?" they asked
But the answer wasn't one that they approved of
So, they made her the object of their ridicule
While she sat in a corner, scoffed.

But before you know, this is Here and Now
When times have changed, as have lives and stories
Scoffers and sceptics are left lamenting
Those who stood apart are worthy of many glories
You may not be what the world wants you to be
You may not say what the world expects you to
Normalcy be damned, you'll stay victorious
If you just listen to one voice: You.

STAY SARCASTIC

Yes, we love the pretty people
The ones with shiny hair and eyes
But they lack the sass, they're a pain in the ass
Because they're so literal and nicey-nice.
The eternal optimists and their motivation
Much like a gooey chocolate cake
You may like it once a day, but you secretly pray
That their smileys won't offset a headache.

It's imperative to meet the ones with wit
The ones who won't bat an eyelid
The ones who'll make you laugh, straight-faced
The ones whose one-liners with acid are laced
The ones who shun the thought of slapstick
The ones who stay blessedly sarcastic.

True, there are people who laugh easily
At stuff that's repetitive and mediocre
Whose idea of fun, is the most basic pun
It's like hanging with a self-confessed joker.
Less said about those who're annoyingly verbose
Nothing can be expressed in less than a para
Our minds may wander, way over yonder
But they'll continue unashamed and blah-blah.

That's when you need to say less
And make a point with much finesse
That's when your brain tingles with a response
That's not too laboured, tinged with nonchalance
That's when you know it's simply fantastic
When you can safely stay blessedly sarcastic.

Here's a quick note to novices of the Art
If you don't get the joke, take heart
Forgive us for not being overenthusiastic
We're simply blessed to stay sarcastic.

NOT A NICE PERSON TO KNOW

It's been ages since we met
You've gone from stubborn to resilient
And pulled through it all
I've gone from juvenile to jaded
And barely survived the fall
You've turned around things with a smile
And dissed the Art of Sadness
I've just laughed and cried quite easily
And bartered calm for madness.

This You is far more brilliant
This Me is far more shallow
So, what can I say that's not been said before
I'm just not a nice person to know.

Time changes all, so they say
You found a balance that's effortless
While shaking up the stagnant
I made changes for a big persona
Then got left with fragments

Your goodness leaves a trail of smiles
It's certain you're unforgettable
My edge has lost its reason
It's definitely regrettable.

This You is far more spectacular
This Me is far more hollow
So, what can I say that's not been said before
I'm just not a nice person to know.

I DON'T LIVE THERE ANYMORE

We were picking fruits
Just green and red
All around
It was like as if
Heaven was our playground
And then, there was blood
Gunshots in my head
That deafening sound
What have we found?
I wonder now
What have we lost
What have we found?

Home
It haunts me in my dream
But I don't live there anymore
Not that I care so much
Because I don't really live anymore.
Home
It throbs in my heart and head
But I don't live there anymore
Not that I care so much
Because I don't really live anymore.

Father locked the gates
But he never looked back
And the orchards said goodbye
The skies wept
Years have passed
And yet, we can't accept
We don't belong there
We don't belong here either
We belong to past perfect
What have we found?
I wonder now
What have we lost
What have we found?

Home
It stalks me in my dream
But I don't live there anymore
Not that I care so much
Because I don't really live anymore.
Home
It throbs in my heart and head
But I don't live there anymore
Not that I care so much
Because I don't really live anymore.

FEELING QUITE DISCO

Things haven't been going so well
Your smile is just for show
You'd been building big plans
Before reality struck a blow.

Everyone reckons you're doing fine
But that's because they don't know
It's not easy to laugh like the breeze
When your song has lost tempo.

And yet, you may just break this wall
And yet, you're feeling quite Disco
And yet, you may just take this fall
And yet, you're feeling quite Disco
Up and down we go
Feeling quite Disco
Starting crazy, then going slow
Yet feeling quite Disco.

You're not listening to what others say
Because words, they're laced with falsetto
Expectations, like fetuses in your brain
Should never be allowed to grow.

Every new day should bring new meaning
And every evening an afterglow
Who says that doors can't be slammed shut
Before you force open a new window.

And yet, a new person may awaken
And yet, you're feeling quite Disco
And yet, an old story may re-open
And yet, you're feeling quite Disco
Up and down we go
Feeling quite Disco
Starting crazy, then going slow
Yet feeling quite Disco.

HANG ON

How happy will you be
Once you've seen breath-taking sunsets
In all the far-flung places
How proud will you feel
Once you've seen looks of adoration
On all the pretty faces
How content will it make you
Once you've finished ticking off everything
That make up your bucket list
How rich will you become
Once you establish you've done better
Than everyone in your midst.

This world will keep tempting you with more
This world will keep offering new
And yet, when you die alone
You'll have only some things to hold on to
Keep hanging on to them, my friend
Keep hanging on
By a thread, by a whisper, by a hope
For what are you when they're gone?

How nice will you become
Once you've said all the right things
To all the right people
How devout a person will you be
Once you've sought the blessings
Of every church and every temple
How seriously will you be taken
Once you've built a home
And filled it up with artefacts
How simple do you think you are
Once you've done your kind deeds
Just to see how the world reacts.

This world will keep teasing you with baubles
This world will keep selling you Brand New
And yet, when you die alone
You'll have only some things to hold on to
Keep hanging on to them, my friend
Keep hanging on
By a thread, by a whisper, by a hope
For what are you when they're gone?

WATERPROOFED

Rain will seep in
Without a sound
And do its damage
Then you'll wake up
See the mess
And think you'll manage.

Fixing the cracks
Has never been easy
So, prepare to deal
With unrest and uneasy
This is the part
When you'll realize the pain
And the pleasure
Of being wet in the rain.

Can you ever be waterproofed
Can you ever have a safety net
Can you ever be so insulated
That you live to forget.

Wind-chimes will clatter
Raindrops will tease the panes
And you'll introspect
Damp shadows will form
In the corners of your mind
When you retrospect.

Thunderstorms are tricky
They come without informing
The nights will be rough
The days won't be heartwarming
This is the part
When you'll realize the extent
Of what was meant to be
And how things went.

Can you ever be waterproofed
Can you ever have a safety net
Can you ever be so insulated
That you live to forget.

LOVE, ALL OVER AGAIN

This world is a smaller place
When we're the only two around
It's always a noisy planet
But I can't seem to hear a sound
Hesitation is just a comma
In a tale not so long-wound
Are those castles in my head
Or is euphoria underground?

I jump in, no safety net
And I meet rainbows and the rain
The passion and the pain
The madness and the sane
The grief and the gain
This is love
All over again.
This is love
All over again.

There's no sun shining
But warmth has occupied its place
There's no song playing
But melody has left a trace
Are we going to take a moment

Before we cut to black
Let's turn up the dial on Crazy
Then make our own soundtrack.

I jump in, eyes unblinking
And I meet the fatigue and the flame
The charades and the champagne
The bye-byes and the blame
The stagnant and hurricane
This is love
All over again.
This is love
All over again.

UNCOMMON CHEMISTRY

Your silences can be louder
Than the weight of my words
And when it comes to conversations
My participation is two-thirds
But there's no co-relation
To what's said and what can be
There's just the magic of what I call
Uncommon chemistry.

Everything is not roses
Everything is not poetry
Everything can be held together
By uncommon chemistry.

My spontaneous may just not be
The kind you appreciate
Your staccato may just not be
The one I highly rate
But here we are, and come to think
I'll give you reason to agree
We share the magic of what I call
Uncommon chemistry.

Everything is not exacting
Everything is not geometry
Everything is strung together
By uncommon chemistry.

We may not ever figure
What's right and what's not to be
And then I could swiftly turn from friend
To an unwilling adversary
But if that's to happen, let us admit
It may just be momentary
Yet we're still held together
By uncommon chemistry.

THE VOICES IN MY HEAD

The voices, the voices in my head
You keep me alive, when I'm long since dead.

Still talking, still mocking
Still asking me questions my conscience finds shocking
Still shining the torch on dingy corners of my mind
Still screaming, still accusing when I choose to turn blind
Still taunting me with regrets, still opening wounds unexposed
Still making me guilty of cases long closed.

The voices, the voices in my head
You keep me alive, when I'm long since dead.

Still giggling, still laughing
Still childlike, before the world came down crashing
Still kind, still benevolent, still looking firmly north
Still reassuring, when I passionately go forth
Still being my friend in need, when I tend to falter
Still shaking up my core when my I'm an emotional defaulter.

The voices, the voices in my head
You keep me alive, when I'm long since dead.

Shake me, debase me
Kill me, embrace me
Through life and death, we'll always be wed
The voices, the voices in my head.

BEING SIMPLE

There's always a choice to make
To say what you mean
And mean what you say
To reply with "I'll see you soon"
But not stagger it everyday
To expect much less
Than your heart anticipates
To find much more
Than your wallet dictates
To give up on fights
That never lead anywhere
To embrace the 'what if'
That comes when you care.

Being simple isn't tough
But yet, it's not a piece of cake
Everything may just work out
And everything may just break
Being simple isn't tough
But then, there's so much at stake
So, whether you win or lose
It's a choice that you make.

There's always a choice to make
To love without expectation
And lose control when being kissed
To trust in your neighbour
And travel without a list
To leave the nightmares behind
When a dream comes to stay
To shake off the ghosts
When you've lived a better day
To acknowledge wisdom
And a warning in the same measure
To treat old friendships
Like one treats guarded treasure.

Being simple isn't tough
And yet, it's not easy to do it
You may just crack it open
And you may just stand to ruin it
Being simple isn't tough
But then, there's so much at stake
So, whether you win or lose
It's a choice that you make.

FEARLESS

Just to be able to feel
And not be scared to show it
Just to be able to love
And not be afraid to know it
Just to be brave enough to cry
And be happy for the salvation tears bring
Just to wake up and think of trying
When another year won't change a thing
What are we if we're not human
If we can't hurt and burn in a cesspool of mess
What are we if we're not human
If we can't fail and fall, then stand fearless.

Fearless
It's not what I thought I could be
Not someone I became willingly
Yet something within me stirred
From a dove I turned firebird
And while I may not have much courage to give
Fearless is how I choose to live.

Just to be able to smile
When tears blur the vision of your brain
Just to be a little bit kinder
When your laughter hides the panic of pain
Just to say what's in your heart
When your world is bursting with white noise
Just to hold on to your dignity
When your action has lost all semblance of poise
What are we if we're not human
If we don't put everything at stake, yet still end with less
What are we if we're not human
If we can't stumble and surrender, then stand fearless.

Fearless
It's not what I thought I could be
Not someone I became willingly
Yet something within me stirred
From a dove I turned firebird
And while I may not have much courage to give
Fearless is how I choose to live.

THIS IS YOU, YOU ARE MAY

It's May
Hot and humid and disorienting
I hallucinate and that's comforting
Of beds of ice and igloos in the sky
Of winds gone berserk and thunderstorms in July
Of sail boats and chiffon and all things Kygo
Of comic books and giggles, childhood, and mango
And just when my imagination begins to sway
The air conditioner groans, we're back to May.

May, you'll do good to remember
You're neither June nor December
But there's something about your clime
That evokes both love and crime
And just like the disparity that's Bombay
This is You; you are May.

It's May
Steeped in slumber, sweat and slackening
Yet my febrile brain has thoughts maddening
Of muslins and margaritas and streets of marigold
Of love that's unbridled and kisses uncontrolled
Of shaping the day like a potter without a plan

Of throwing caution to the winds, like a young catamaran
And just when my imagination begins to sway
The air conditioner groans, we're back to May.

May, you'll do good to remember
You're neither June nor December
But there's something about your clime
That evokes both love and crime
And just like the disparity that's Bombay
This is You; you are May.

YOU'RE NOT THAT PERSON ANYMORE

You've been robbed
And left to deal with it
There isn't a vestige of who you were
Your yesterdays are a cobweb of blur
The person who sang simple songs in his head
Is now a thousand dreams and sins ahead
You're not that person anymore
That person is certainly dead.

You've been compromised
And told to be normal
There isn't a line you haven't crossed
Or a promise you've not taken and tossed
The person whose tears cleansed the rain
And whose smile melted away the pain
You're not that person anymore
That person won't return again.

You've been shot
And asked to live with it
There isn't a day you've pushed Mediocre
Or gone out of the way to figure what broke her

The person whose love was stronger than conviction
And whose judgement was the strongest validation
You're not that person anymore
That person is now pure fiction.

COFFEE ISN'T EVERYONE'S CUP OF TEA

I've been meaning to ask you a lot of questions
But somehow, I've not been able to get there
Because my questions aren't altogether logical
They lack pattern and land from anywhere
And then, you counteract all the madness I own
By conducting a very droll enquiry
It's not like you have to get used to this
Because coffee isn't everyone's cup of tea.

We may not get along, but we may as well do
For there's a long journey we've got to cover
And no matter how much you take umbrage
You'll find my opinions are like no other
I'm trying to be a little guarded but then
That's just not how I am meant to be
It's not like you have to get used to this
Because coffee isn't everyone's cup of tea.

A shining example of method, you lack finesse
But then, that's not an opinion you uphold
And when you say I'm not quite that mature
I can tell that you think I'm uncontrolled
It's going to be difficult to make you see this
Because your viewpoint is a bit finicky
It's not like you have to get used to this
Because coffee isn't everyone's cup of tea.

WEPT

They won't hurt you here, he said
But in the end, all she did was bled
And the stories continued to spread.

Posts were written, anger was displayed
Some agitated, some fervently prayed
But sadly, justice was denied and delayed.

They say that such things take time to end
They say that punishment may not make amends
But who's to say - if they'll break or we'll bend.

The voices will get louder, anger will rise
But all of us are wondering, if this alone will suffice
For the fault lies in us, we must pay the price.

We may worship the deities, but inside us lies black
We may walk to temples, but its humanity we lack
And for all of that, we must face the flack.

This isn't us, this is the story of a nation
This problem lies within, it's our own creation
So, let's not treat it like a tumour, in isolation.

When we get to the root, we'll see the rot
How impoverished we are, in mind and thought
And how much little we were really taught.

We all have crosses to bear, this is ours to accept
The fact that as a society, we're morally inept
And somewhere close by, another girl has wept.

LONER

What gave you the idea
That I was a loner
Was I looking sufficiently busy
Staring at my phone, quite pretentious
Or was I doing that chatter
That's largely noise, wholly pointless
Or was I laughing too loud
At jokes that weren't meant to be funny
Or did I stand at the bar
And eavesdrop on conversations, quite openly.

It's funny you should tell me
Because I noticed you as well
You weren't looking like you were happy
Don't ask but I could tell.

What gave me the idea
That you were a loner
Were you hobnobbing with a crowd of people
All collectively glad you're there
Or was it the fact that in a matter of time
They were around, but you didn't care
Or was it the silent plea for help

That surrounds each brave word you speak
Or the dystopia that you battle with
When you show up at work and leave.

It's funny I should tell you
Because you noticed me as well
I wasn't looking like I was happy
I won't ask but you can tell.

ON OPINIONS

Some of our opinions are hasty
Some are not really bold
Some are just plain distasteful
But they're still ours to own.

They're ours to flaunt unbridled
Or carefully hide in heart
They're ours to showcase cleverly
When you scale the popularity chart.

Some are biased, some neutral
And some are laced with desperate fear
Some call themselves opinion makers
Though their intentions may be unclear.

And then there's a tribe, quite sadly
Who in fact, have no opinions
They're happy to nod and say yes to all
Rather than be the cat among pigeons.

Opinions have a way of defining us
And building a thing called perspective
Have some, take some, give some
But in the end, just live and let live.

ABOUT A CHAT

I haven't told you so much
Even though I've told you so much
Like how I'm fond of cinnamon
And keep a tiny piece in my wallet
Or how I watch a thousand dog videos
And imagine their voice-overs in my head
Or how I obsess over my morning tea
But don't eat enough to keep healthy
It's all there, this stuff that makes me
This stuff that breaks me
But whenever you ask me what's up
I just say 'nothing much'
We should chat.
Really, we should chat.

I haven't told you so much
Even though I've told you so much
Like how I love jackfruit and guava
And dislike goddamn gourds
Or how I always doodle concentric circles
Whenever I'm trying to concentrate
Or how I grieve that love may elude me
And life may delude me

It's all there, this stuff that makes me
This stuff that breaks me
But whenever you ask me what's up
I just say 'nothing much'
We should chat.
Really, we should chat.

HOME: THE REASON

I enter, switch on the fairy lights
And suddenly there's an inner glow in the darkness
The wind chimes aren't even moving
Yet there's a beautiful lilt in their calmness
I make a cup of tea, there's no sugar
But there's a comfort I can't quite fathom
The cookies, they're just cookies from a pack
But somehow, they taste of compassion.

Home. It's so much more than a feeling.
It's like I found a reason
To be the person I'm in my heart
Born to be safe, yet bred in freedom.

The music's on, it's a foreign tune
But it's a rhythm that lifts my spirit
I look outside, concrete hides the trees
But the moon still looks so vivid
Dinner's not so tempting, but that's okay
For there's enough to fill my soul
It's just another day when I've got back home
But I feel stirred, yet in control.

Home. It's so much more than a feeling.
It's like I found a reason
To be the person I'm in my heart
Born to be safe, yet bred in freedom.

DYSFUNCTIONAL

My mamma ain't the mamma
That a mamma ought to be
My Daddy's got some stories
That won't gain him sympathy
My sisters and my brothers
They're just looking for a fight
My point of view is coloured
It's blacker than it's white.

There's a word for people like us
Is it dysfunctional
But what you fail to notice
Is we're paradoxical
There's a word for people like us
Is it dysfunctional
And no matter what you call us
We're still unstoppable.

There's not a wound we've closed
Without abusing the cure
There's not a truth we've harvested
Without taking a detour
And in between the shame and pride

We create our own utopia
Then when things come shattering down
We shape it into disturbia.

There's a word for people like us
Is it dysfunctional
But what you fail to notice
Is we're indestructible
There's a word for people like us
Is it dysfunctional
And no matter what you call us
We're still unstoppable.

THERE'S A NEW WORLD CALLING

There's a new world that's calling
You and me and all of us
It's going easy on what society thinks
It's laughing out loud at the fuss.

There's a new world that's calling
One where your gold and money won't matter
What will set you apart is how you embrace
A stranger, a neighbour and a daughter.

There's a new world that's calling
It's asking why not and how soon
Questions are being asked, tables are being turned
And God is sounding a bit out of tune.

There's a new world that's calling
And points of view are getting radical
Fundamentalists are on the rise and somehow
Every harmless joke is now inflammable.

There's a new world that's calling
A frenetic mess, a constant crusade
But yet, it's momentarily fun, it's coming undone
It's a world that you and I made.

SAYING NO

Shaking my head is becoming a habit
Because I feel like a No is coming up
And it's not like I'm wired that way
But saying No is easier than whassup.

I'm turning out to be a little smarter
And No is becoming a close ally
Conversations are becoming emptier, as are silences
It's really more Okay than a Why.

It's easy being a Yes Man, you should know it
But being a No Woman isn't easier
I wish sarcasm wasn't my shadow
I sincerely wish for you, I was breezier.

Announcing my intentions is straightforward
And that's all that you really need to know
And may I offer some worthy advice here
Saying no is easier, no?

WE STILL HAVE NEXT YEAR

We still have next year
To write a brand-new love letter
A whole new year
To shape our understanding of Better.

We still have next year
To break free of the slavery
A whole 365 days
To come to terms with bravery.

We still have next year
To trash feeble excuses and find a reason
A whole lot of new stories
That will kick start a brand-new season.

It's never going to be too good or too bad
It's never going to be too brilliant or too blue
You're never going to feel life is too fair
You're never going to feel that something special's in the air
But there's still a reason to be somewhat new
And that could just lie inside of you.

DOSE OF DISTRACTION

Some things are easily fixed
Some things take a little more time
You can't always ponder and retreat
You don't always land a gold mine
But no matter what your force of habit
No matter what your scene of crime
I'm just here to give you a reason
To make you feel a little bit fine.

Dose of Distraction
You need a dose of distraction
There's a heartbeat skipping somewhere
There's a force of attraction
Dose of Distraction
You need a dose of distraction
I've got a tingling feeling here
There's a force of attraction.

Up close, it may not hold to reason
And you can choose to analyze it
Thus far, there is no punctuation
But a comma will only paralyze it
Regret may come a bit later

And you can always call yourself a fool
I'm just here to make you happy
When you break your own ground rule.

Dose of Distraction
You need a dose of distraction
There's a heartbeat skipping somewhere
There's a force of attraction
Dose of Distraction
You need a dose of distraction
I've got a tingling feeling here
There's a force of attraction.

EATING AND SLEEPING

Eating and sleeping
They're like partners in crime
One follows the other, most willing
So lethargically sublime.

How can one not like the two
Because the two sure like each other
And just as soon as you've eaten big
You feel the creeping up of slumber.

Food and sleep, sleep and food
Stomach leads, yawn follows
And inevitably when you have no time
You die for bed and pillows.

Some are lucky, they get siesta
Some others have to stay up with coffee
Not too fair, because eating demands
The indulgence of all things sleepy.

Eating and sleeping, oh you little joys
You bring meaning to our lives, so roundabout
Because you add further pleasure to gastronomy
With the joy of wanting to pass out.

BEAUTIFUL STRANGER

When I think how
I knew you like the back of my hand
I second-guessed everything you'd have planned
And now it's all in the past
Not that we thought it would last
But that's the imminent danger
Of knowing you, Beautiful Stranger.

When I think how
We were listening to the same music lately
And creating some of our own, sedately
And now, we're quite out of tune
The sun is too bright for the moon
But that's the imminent danger
Of knowing you, Beautiful Stranger.

When I think how
We pulled through days filled with Woelfuls
And smiled through them all with our Hopefuls
And now, we're not seeing any rainbows
Barely are we even in the same flow
But that's the imminent danger
Of knowing you, Beautiful Stranger.

When I think how
We created a whole new dictionary
One that was sweet, funnily visionary
And now, these words, they seem staccato
And conversations run on Mode Auto
But that's the imminent danger
Of knowing you, Beautiful Stranger.

SEA, YOU, ME

Unless you have
Something to say
Something that will
Define this day
Unless you have
Something to ask
Something that will
Lift my mask
It's just going to be
The sea, you and me
For when was the last time
You set a date with
Infinity?

A slice of heaven
An expanse of sea
It's all right here
A glimpse of you and me
So why do the asking
Why do the tasking
We'll let these sands
Present us eternity.

Until we have
That mystery
The kind that comes from
Pure chemistry
Until we have
That synergy
The kind that comes from
Shared history
It's just going to be
The sea, you and me
For when was the last time
You set a date with
Infinity?

A slice of heaven
An expanse of sea
It's all right here
A glimpse of you and me
So why do the asking
Why do the tasking
We'll let these sands
Present us eternity.

DROWNING

I am used to drowning
It's what I do
Sometimes without reason
Because it's easier to gasp for breath
Than grapple with reality.

I want to come up for air
I want to
It's what I want
But not what I do.

I am used to drowning
It's what I do
Floating meaninglessly through slime
While it takes me down under
And I feel happier to resign.

I want to come up for air
I want to
It's what I want
But not what I do.

I am used to drowning
It's what I do
Countering tides, fighting sharks
While I desperately beat around
For a hint of comeback.

I want to come up for air
I want to
It's what I want
But not what I do.

DYING TO BE FOUND

You can be so smart
And you can dance as well
But when it comes to telling
If we both will gel.

You just have no clue
And you probably won't try
To give us a chance in hell
Because you're wondering why.

So, here's the thing, and it's sudden
But just as soon as we meet
There's a trip in my heartbeat
It's both scary and sweet.

Then I feel quite speechless
Then I feel quite unprepared
You're just so bold and unfazed
And yet, so beautifully layered.

So, I'll just keep this short
Fallen leaves make no sound
Maybe you can't hear me
But I'm dying to be found.

Dying to be found
Dying to be found
For fallen leaves make sound.

C'EST LA VIE

Yes, I've travelled far, not wide
And had my share of troubles
Yes, I've compromised clear thought
To the joy of uncommon muddles
Yes, I've loved and lost and tossed it all
And created quite the flutter
I've earned that corner office they wanted
And celebrated with pretty clutter.

And yet, there's nothing I have done
That has made me feel more human
There's no story I have told
That's been told and gotten proven
C'est La Vie, darling, C'est La Vie
What did we do with the days gone by
Where have they gone, what will become
And why does my heart still cry.

Yes, I've pleased the ones who mattered
And the one who tried to get closer
I've made myself quite available
Wherever I could be the poser
Yes, I've quelled the burning light

That was inside me, bright and burning
I've given in to those nights
Which come with no prior warning.

And yet, there's nothing I have done
That has made me feel more human
There's no story I have told
That's been told and gotten proven
C'est La Vie, darling, C'est La Vie
What did we do with the days gone by
Where have they gone, what will become
And why does my heart still cry.

TIED IN HOLY MATRIMONY

'Are you mad?', she asked
Over a hushed whisper and a glare
'Whatever gave you the idea' he replied
And studiously ignored her stare.

She wasn't good at sparring
He wasn't good at being slighted
They weren't too happy a couple
But yet, they sat there united.

It was apparent to all who saw them
That they were tied in holy matrimony
But anyone who glanced at them closer
Could tell their dalliance was phony.

They suffered the silences, ate their words
And came out a little bit defeated
And yet, they proudly wore the badge
Of never having bedded and cheated.

It wasn't sensational, it wasn't original
And yet, it was telling of the time
When neither one cared, yet no one dared
To leave what they considered a shrine.

FIGHTER

You think you won't survive
It's not like you've done before
You've been waking up every morning
Only to be shown the exit door
But there's a truth to every lie
There's a force you can't deny
And it's in your smile, it's in your tear
It's in every day you bravely get by

Fighters aren't born, they're made
Everyone who's brave, has been afraid
You may be more wrong than a righter
But that doesn't mean you're not a fighter
Show us the fighter
You know how it's done
Show us the fighter
Fight, till you've won.

How will the voices subside
How will the ghosts die down
How will the stories you're writing end
When you live in Darkness Town
But there's something you didn't account for

There's something you underestimated
It's in your heart, and it's blazing
It's the fighter in you, interrupted.

Fighters aren't born, they're made
Everyone who's brave, has been afraid
You may be more wrong than a righter
But that doesn't mean you're not a fighter
Show us the fighter
You know how it's done
Show us the fighter
Fight, till you've won.

MAYBE, YOU CAN SET IT RIGHT

Maybe you've told too many lies
And maybe you've hurt too many people
Maybe you've not undone your mistakes
Maybe your heart has been too fickle
Maybe your life won't take a turn
Maybe you won't get that second chance
Maybe your job won't get any better
And maybe you'll be spurned by romance.

But tonight, let your heartbeats be shiny
Tonight, let your eyes dazzle with light
For this is the Festival of Wonder
And maybe, only you can set it right.

Maybe you expect too much from everyone
Maybe they're right in calling you crazy
Maybe your plans to quit won't happen
Maybe you'll always be just this lazy
Maybe your weight will always stress you
Maybe your good-hair days won't last
Maybe the last laugh won't be yours to have
And maybe you won't outdo the past.

But tonight, let your heartbeats be shiny
Tonight, let the stars be your guiding light
For this is the Festival of Wonder
And maybe, only you can set it right.

A LOVE SONG OF THE YOUNG

Are we allowed to talk in a cinema
I don't think so, but I want to ask you
That if I thought this movie was boring
Would you still allow me to call you
You've been looking so wonder struck
And I can't help but feel a tinge of envy
Because the action sucks, so does the dialogue
And the plot is beyond mercy.

But all that won't matter
If we get over the idle chatter
Let me take your hand and we'll linger
While you wrap me around your li'l finger
They say that love is waning
In a world where apathy is reigning
But for me, the world has stopped to matter
Since we started our idle chatter.

You can choose to be all articulate
But I'm just not equipped to match you
So, if I say things that are just clumsy
Would you know the truth is, I worship you
I'm just a young lad, you'll laugh me off

There's not a clever retort I can give back
But when it comes to depth of my feeling
You'll be amazed, I'm quite the maniac.

But all that won't matter
If we get over the idle chatter
Let me take your hand and we'll linger
While you wrap me around your li'l finger
They say that love is waning
In a world where apathy is reigning
But for me, the world has stopped to matter
Since we started our idle chatter.

ICHI-GO ICHI-E

Ichi-go ichi-e is a Japanese idiom that describes a cultural concept of treasuring meetings with people. The term is often translated as "for this time only," "never again," or "one chance in a lifetime." It reminds people to cherish any gathering that they may take part in, citing the fact that many meetings in life are not repeated.

Here we are
Two strangers in the bar
Just having our drink, a quiet think
And you say something weird
It's something I haven't heard
So, you share it, I layer it
And we have a conversation
What it's about is secondary
But in the moment, it's magical
And so, it goes
The night and the encounter
You, Me, Us.

Ichi-go ichi-e
For this time only
We can be the best we want to be
Maybe we'll never ever meet

But that thought should take back seat
Ichi-go ichi-e
For this time only.

Here we are
Separated by colour and age
United by chance and encounter
In one faraway place
So, what if we lie
So, what if we tell a tall story
It will all add up
To a bubble of remembrance
Embedded in head and heart
That can never be replicated
Maybe that's why it's stunning
Me, You, Us.

Ichi-go ichi-e
For this time only
We can be the best we want to be
Maybe we'll never ever meet
But that thought should take back seat
Ichi-go ichi-e
For this time only.

A SHORT POEM ABOUT DEATH

Always been kissed
Never been missed
She'd spent a life most ordinary
Always been laid
Never been craved
That was her everyday story
So, she decided to fuck it
And simply kicked the bucket
It was then that she got noticed
Now her Facebook is pouring
With eulogies enduring
Death has been her passport to Lived.

CON ARTIST

So, you think I'm creative
Vivid and Imaginative
Maybe I am all of that, so hence
I'm putting up a good pretense
Of being a woman quite remarkable
And bold and blah blah-able
But if you're so blinded by the show
Let's put it to test, and you'll know.

Con artist, there's a con artist in me
Con artist, I'll be what you want me to be
Con artist, makeup, and make-believe
Con artist, I still got a trick up my sleeve.

If there's a show to be done, I'll do it
If there's a wound to be covered, I'll glue it
In real, I may not be so appealing
And what I say, I may not be feeling
What matters is whether I can display
A finer definition of human decay
And each time, I mouth what I have often said
You can be sure a part of me is dead.

Con artist, there's a con artist in me
Con artist, I'll be what you want me to be
Con artist, makeup, and make-believe
Con artist, I still got a trick up my sleeve.

EXCUSES

Excuses are pretty little things.
Pretty and fragile
And made up of well-told lies
That float around in cocoons of altered-reality.

Altered is a good reality, you alter it
And when you choose, you un-alter it.
But make no mistake about excuses
These are spineless and weepy creatures.
Unable to stand up and fight
For the shadow of the person you're pretending to be
So just as you clutch on to them
They'll let go and make you the problem.

So, one day,
This excuse becomes your story
And all that remains of you
Is a pathetic bag of excuses.

AND THEN THERE WERE TWO

Are you listening?
Said the heart to the head
I'm sick and tired of being told
That you're the reason we are in shreds
I'm weary of carrying the burden
Of being flimsy and fluctuating
But that's not entirely my fault
Because you're so damn calculating.

Are you listening?
Said the head to the heart
You're nothing but a big old fool
And that doesn't translate into smart
If I'd been you, I'd have thrown in the towel
But you're a dreamer, that's the pity
And here's a wake-up call you may hate
But you don't make us look too pretty.

Are you listening?
Said the mind to them both
We're all of us in this together
So, stop passing the blame, it's all in the game
One can't predict rough weather.
And so, they went and lived again
As mind and heart and head
And even though they made peace that day
One of them, soon just dropped dead.

THIS IS (NOT) THAT MOMENT

This is that moment
When you can choose to be the moss
Wet, dark, and mushy
Or that sunflower
Flapping happy, in the sunshine.

This is that moment
When you can brim with the knowledge
Of being able to create a New Something
Or stumble in the grimness
Of being the Original Nothing.

This is that moment
When you can live your greatest love story
And have nobody feature in it but you
Or you can become the victim of a chapter
That's pathetically crowded with pathos.

This is that moment
When you can overcome the insults
And build a bridge of Doubtless
Or revel in the ignominy
And wade in a lake of Thoughtless.

This is that moment
But you know this and so do I
That Change is not a Painkiller
While Grief is a Sedative.

You know this and so do I
That being a bigger person
Is something you like seeing in the movies
But you, you can never do it.

You know this and so do I
That you don't want to break this loop
Of moments that roll into one another
You don't want to be what you're capable of
Because that requires conviction
And this is not that moment.

BIG, BAD CITY: THE SONG OF COURAGE

What's the point of being so available
When availability is no antidote to loneliness
What's the point of being so grateful
When you can't redeem it for kindness
Sure, such thoughts could be a reason
To run away and take refuge in pity
But hey, let it be a reason to stay
And make it in this big, bad city
Show us your courage
Show us you're gritty
Show us you're bringing it down
In this, in this big, bad city.

What's the point of being so edgy
When your edge is just making you pretentious
What's the point of being in love
When all your love is just shallow and facetious
Sure, such thoughts can be a reason
To run away and blame it on the Almighty
But hey, let it be a reason to stay
And make it in this big, bad city
Show us your courage
Show us you're gritty
Show us you're bringing it down
In this, in this big, bad city.

MAKING IT, BREAKING IT

Hey, there's nothing so bad
About being a bit of a mess
I think everyone's got a U-turn to take
And that may involve some stress
Sure, some find it easy
To dance a bit, sing a tune
Some tell a joke, then laugh the loudest
But frankly, I'm immune.

All in a day's work,
All in a day's play
This is the way we flow
This is never going away.
All in a day's work,
All in a day's play
This is how it all works
This is how it all goes away.

Hey, there's nothing so bad
About being a little too fussed
In creating a patch of sunshine
That's eventually going to go bust

Sure, some find it easy
To fuck it up, then pretend they're sinking
Some make plans, then rubbish them
Quite honestly, I'm beyond thinking.

All in a day's work,
All in a day's play
This is the way we flow
This is never going away.
All in a day's work,
All in a day's play
This is how it all works
This is how it all goes away.

PMS GODDESS

Could I bite someone's head off?
And then wash it down with four beers
Could I not feel so sick and bloated
And could my eyes not well up with tears?

Could my stomach stop being a living revolt
And my mood be less cantankerous
Could I not crave caffeine topped with dessert
And binge-watch a show most amorous.

My interest in happy things seems to wane
And I develop an unhealthy tendency to mourn
But then, I talk to ladies who sadly tell me
That I'm not in this battle alone.

So, for all those goddesses who're PMSed
Here's a nice bright cheery thought
When your chums end and you feel thinner
We'll talk about being divas and what not.

CRAZY COCKTAIL GIRL

She was like that crazy cocktail
you order on impulse
The one you have one or two of
and then decide to go back
To the tried and tested.

All she ever wants
Is to become that whisky drink
The one you savour every evening
The one that comforts you on a Monday
And yet, excites you on a Friday night.

But she remains trapped
In the exotic and erotic
While deep down
Her still waters run deep
Waiting for a boat
To float sublimely on it.

There isn't a tale
That's not a juxtaposition
Of expectation and reality
And so, hers is just another
Another dazzling irony.

All hail this crazy cocktail
Who craves much more
But remains just that
The madness you desire
But rarely need.

MUSINGS OF VALENTINO
PART 1

This journey has started
You and I
And we don't have a destination
But that's how the best trips play out.
Don't they?

We'll soar and fly
Even though some may take to walking
And then, when others gaze at the moon
We'll just stare endlessly at the night
And go, Oh My!

Then when the clouds gather
We'll seek a roof and start a fire
One that may not be all that talked about
But we'll be warm in the moment
Won't we?

So, won't you join me
And take this road together
Tomorrow may not be too far away
But today is brilliant weather
Come on!

MUSINGS OF VALENTINO
PART 2

In your eyes
I see desperation
The kind that's bit agony-aunt, bit agony
And a pathetic kind of longing
I want to hide.

In your arms
I see clinging
The kind that's begging to be held
Yet strangely, has no hold on me
I want to run.

In your feet
I see chains
The kind you want to put on me
It's weighing me down already
I want to scream.

In your company
I see boredom
The kind that settles in like fat
And doesn't dissolves easily
I want to throw up.

In your love
I see nothing
Nothing that I want to see
Nothing that I want to share
I want to die.

THE DEMON WITHIN

Most days, you stay hidden
Well concealed by layers of nicety
And then on a day like any other
You emerge, with all your ferocity.

Dark and brooding, dirty and conniving
Mean and vicious, greedy and suspicious
Ugly, selfish, unkind, pessimistic
Wicked, wanton, snarky, narcissistic.

And suddenly, you've turned me inside out
And I scream 'that's not me, get out'
But you smile and say "Hello there, you know me well"
And all I can do is beg you to go to hell.

And I wonder if this is true of all
For years, we've been staying within society's walls
We say the right things, act gracious
While what we may feel, is far outrageous.

So, we'll wear our nice clothes and wash our pretty face
And then go out, and say we love this place
We love the world, we love each other
And we want to thank everyone, from our phone to our mother.

While sleeping inside us, a demon will awake
The darkness of which will make our conscience quake
O Darker Soul, O Demon Heart
Stay away from me, till death do us apart.

GYPSY GIRL, SING ME A SONG

Sing me a song, girl on a tree
Hanging from the branches
Your hair let loose; your heart set free
Tell me about the hopes that you hang on to
The ones others mock you for
Tell me about the dreams you lost along the way
But you still stare at from afar
Tell me about the times you felt cold and lost
But you wore your old socks and laughed with wine
Tell me about the days when everyone was chasing things
But you were happy not waiting for a sign
Tell me all your stories, O Gypsy Girl
For you lived in me, once long ago
And when you left, it was a sad long day
You haven't returned since and I don't blame you
For your home is haunted now by delusion
Trifle jokes, meaningless and boredom
That girl is gone, so is the meandering
And all that's left is a plea.
So, sing me a song, girl on the tree.

UNDILUTED

I'm not so sure about a spritzer
Soda in wine is not my style
I'm not so sure about dilution
So, give me the truth straight up, even if it takes a while.

Give me your passion unbridled
Even if it's going to burn
Give me your time undivided
Even if I have to wait my turn.

Give me your shame explicit
Even if it will make you less desirable
Give me your fears un-glossed
Even if it makes you more vulnerable

I'm not so sure about dilution
Because watery is so not worth my while
I'm not so sure about a spritzer
For soda in wine is not my style.

WHEN YOU ARE MY UNIVERSE

The shadows on the wall
They're getting longer
And our connections maybe
They're getting stronger
Finding a corner in my head
Is easier than you imagined
Standing a chance with you
Is nicer un-imagined.

Places we've never been
They'll start growing a road
Phases we've yet to manoeuvre
They'll probably be explored
Too much of talking is a bad thing
Too much of thinking is worse
And procrastination is just evil
When you are my universe.

MAYBE DEFINITELY

Staying grounded is solid
Being whimsical isn't your thing
The last time you threw caution to the winds
Caution came back to sting
And before you could even grimace
You had fallen.

Now, here you are
Quite similarly placed in a situation
And you've been biding your time
Probably weighing your options
But consider the option you've not used so far
Only for a moment do.

Now, don't say you're betting on it
Or even claim that you're being reckless
Just take a deep breath
And leap into what you think is best
For sometimes it is in a Maybe
That you will find a Definitely.

HAPPEN

I've just walked in and am close to bored already
It's not like I expected anything to happen
And then I see you standing there
Dim lit, not so fit
And Happen just happens.

You're looking kind of lost and it's comforting
Because suddenly I'm not so alone
By now, I'm wondering what would happen
 If we said hello, talk some more
What if Happen just happens?

 I've reached the end of my drink, so soon
And there's nothing a lot happening in my head
And hey, you're leaving already
Am I just late or is it just fate
Because Happen just left the building.

SINGLE AGAIN

She's facing the music on her own
Much too long she's been
Dancing to the tune of someone she knew
No longer, she's not too keen

And as she takes in the sights
It's not like she's betraying
But there's a halo around her
That's simply, quite simply saying

Single Again, I'm Single Again
So I'll take that holiday for one
And if you're gonna be my mate
Let's not share anything but fun

She's taking the punches like a pro
It's not like she's not been beaten
But what's the use of a story if you've
Never bitten more than you should've eaten

So, she's got her bagful of worries
But she's not tying it up with a string of Attached
And as she readies to walk it alone
She's saying to you in a tone detached

Single Again, I'm Single Again
So I'll walk with you, do you like walking?
But if you're looking for a heart-to-heart
Get this, I won't be doing the talking.

THE JOURNEY WITHIN

Look at you
So strong, so bullish, so carefree
And yet, you can't see, you can't see it at all
You've been such a mess lately.
The world has stood still in your playground
And you've been grouped into Anonymously
And that's the thing about dreams you nurture long but die fast
They end cruelly.

Look at you
So worn, so wishful, so weary
And yet, you're here and you're surveying this life
And it feels like infinity.
But you choose not to draw the spotlight on you
After all, you've been pretty busy
Fighting the daily wars that take you away from the big battle
And that's a pity.

Look at you
So out there, outspoken, outwardly
And yet, you're not so sure about where to start
Or when to swim against the tide vehemently.
Take my word, let's clear this patch
For past the obscure, you'll spot it quite clearly
That what you thought had passed, has been in you all along
For without conviction, what are we?

TRAVELLER

When I set out to travel
I'll drop the shadow
The shadow of being someone
Someone you or anyone else knows

I'll lie back in the anonymity
And stretch out my possibilities
The possibility that my North Star is on a sabbatical
And my Crazy Star is on the rise

Could I be foolish and yet make you smile?
Could I be mindless and yet come out wise?
Could I wander and yet not be lost?
Could I find a new address that is not home?

Could I swim in an infinity of strangers
And find something to share with each one of them?
Could I do something for the sheer fun of it
And not feel plummeted by the 'what ifs'?

GOSSIP-INSURED

I heard you got too tipsy and trashy
But that's okay, the person who told me is news-flashy
And just when she wanted me to believe otherwise
Her augmented envy hit me between my eyes

Hearsay is hearsay, it's a pity
Gossip is burning up this city
While it's better to be hated than ignored
Who in this world can be Gossip-insured?

I hear you found love in the arms of Mr. Not-so-Right
But that's okay, the person who told me is uptight
And just when his barb reeked of Patronizing
His impish boy-like charm turned agonizing

Hearsay is hearsay, it's a pity
Gossip is burning up this city
While it's a sign of the distantly-matured
Who in this world can be Gossip-insured?

I hear you have an addiction all compelling
But that's okay, the person who told me is repelling
And just when I begin to feel a sense of déjà vu
I figure the rumour involves me, not you

Hearsay is hearsay, it's a pity
Gossip is burning up this city
No smoke without fire, I've heard
Who in this world can be Gossip-insured?